TO

_____

FROM

_____

DATE

_____

MESSAGE

_____

_____

_____

_____

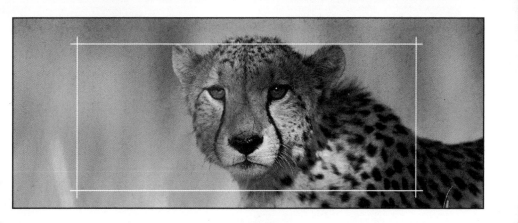

Think on These Things Journal

Compiled from *Think on These Things* by John C. Maxwell © 1999. Published by Beacon Hill Press of Kansas City. A division of Nazarene Publishing House, 2923 Troost, Kansas City, Missouri, 64109, USA.

© 2003 Christian Art Gifts, RSA
        Christian Art Gifts Inc., IL, USA

Compiled by Lynette Douglas
Designed by Christian Art Gifts

EAN 6-006937-05815-6

Printed in China

03   04   05   06   07   08   09   10   11   12   –   10   9   8   7   6   5   4   3   2   1

JOHN MAXWELL

THINK *on these* THINGS

Journal

40 days to renewing your mind

christian
art gifts

INTRODUCTION

How you think determines who you are. Renewing your mind according to the Word of God can change your life. This 40-day journey will help you to renew your thoughts, guiding you to achieve your full potential. Leadership expert, John Maxwell, presents nuggets of wisdom from his best-selling book *Think on These Things* to help you make the most of the potential that God has placed in you. God created you with a specific purpose in mind, a specific plan for your life, and a specific path for you to walk.

As you walk with God, focusing on your life in the light of His Word, and through the insights gained by prayer, you will begin to develop your potential in every area, identify the opportunities the Lord presents to you, adjust your outlook on life, and define success in every area of your life.

Each day of the journey provides you with points to ponder, Scripture verses to reflect on, and steps for faith's action to give you direction, insight and wisdom. Spend time in prayer with the Lord, recording your responses to the questions raised, and His pattern for your life will begin to unfold. Write down your dreams, goals, desires, and ambitions and discover how He delights in bringing all things together for your good, because you love Him and were chosen by Him to bear good fruit.

Our ability to achieve anything great for God begins in our hearts and minds. Pour out your heart to God on these pages, and let Him remind you of His promises for your life. Share your doubts and fears, your longings and desires, your successes and setbacks with Him, and let Him renew your hope, refresh your heart and revive your soul. Begin today to walk into the fullness of the abundant life that God has prepared for you.

May these pages add value to your life, may they help you to focus on what is noble, right, and praiseworthy so that the God of peace will be with you.

S·E·C·T·I·O·N 1

WISDOM FROM
THE WORD

Therefore, if anyone is in Christ,
he is a new creation; the old
has gone, the new has come!
2 Corinthians 5:17

D·A·Y 1
THINK NEW THOUGHTS

THINK ON THESE THINGS

A leader's ability to achieve anything great for God begins in his or her heart and mind.

_____

_____

_____

_____

_____

_____

_____

_____

_____

_____

The good man brings good things out of the good stored up in his heart, and the evil man brings evil things out of the evil stored up in his heart. For out of the overflow of his heart his mouth speaks.

~ Luke 6:45

You can change your life by changing your thinking. You can change your thinking by changing your environment, the use of your free time, and your associations. Use Philippians 4:8 as the guideline to be applied in your thought life. Do your best to make it your standard for selecting friends, filling your free time, and changing your surroundings.

Finally, brothers, whatever is true, whatever is noble, whatever is right, whatever is pure, whatever is lovely, whatever is admirable – if anything is excellent or praiseworthy – think about such things.

~ Philippians 4:8

FAITH'S ACTION:
Think about what
you think about.
Are your thoughts
more positive
than negative, or
do you focus on
the problems you
face? You can
change your life
by changing your
thinking. What in
your life is noble,
true, pure, lovely,
admirable, excellent
and praiseworthy?
Think on these
things.

D·A·Y 2
LOVE AND FAITH

THINK ON THESE THINGS

The love, joy, and peace that Jesus gives when one becomes His child will
without question make a change in any individual's life.

_You love righteousness and hate wickedness; therefore God, your God, has set you
above your companions by anointing you with the oil of joy._

~ Psalm 45:7

Every person needs the faith that will light any path, relieve any distress, bring joy out of sorrow, peace out of strife, and friendship out of enmity.

The only thing that counts is faith expressing itself through love.

~ *Galatians 5:6*

FAITH'S ACTION:
God has promised
you His mercy,
love, peace and joy.
Consider how His
gifts, received in
faith, have changed
your life, and will
continue to do so.

D·A·Y 3
FRUITFULNESS

THINK ON THESE THINGS

Keep your relationship right with God, keep your life disciplined, and with all your strength fulfill God's purpose for your life. Your constant contact with the Vine will make it possible.

"I am the vine; you are the branches. If a man remains in me and I in him, he will bear much fruit; apart from me you can do nothing."

~John 15:5

Those around us know what type of a person we are because of the fruit we bear in our daily living.

But the fruit of the Spirit is love, joy, peace, patience, kindness, goodness, faithfulness, gentleness and self-control (Gal. 5:22-23).

God's purpose for His children is fruitfulness.

"This is to my Father's glory, that you bear much fruit, showing yourselves to be my disciples."
~ *John 15:8*

FAITH'S ACTION:
Does the fruit
in your life bear
evidence of God's
purpose for you?

D·A·Y 4
BARRIER-BREAKERS

THINK ON THESE THINGS

Thank God for the people who are willing to knock holes in roofs. They are pacesetters, the barrier-breakers, the miracle-producers. They are different because they are determined. They're criticized because they're concerned. But most important – they bring people to Jesus.

Some men came, bringing to him a paralytic, carried by four of them. Since they could not get him to Jesus because of the crowd, they made an opening in the roof above Jesus and, after digging through it, lowered the mat the paralyzed man was lying on. When Jesus saw their faith, he said to the paralytic, "Son, your sins are forgiven."

~ Mark 2:3-5

The conviction that only Jesus could take care of their friend's problem gave the men boldness and determination. They could have said, "He's too heavy" or "The crowd's too large" or "We have lost our opportunity." They could have gone home discouraged and missed a miracle – but they refused to quit. The determination of four men meant victory for their friend.

Let us not become weary in doing good, for at the proper time we will reap a harvest if we do not give up.

~ *Galatians 6:9*

FAITH'S ACTION:
How's your deter-
mination? Do you
hold tenaciously
to the promise and
purpose God has
for your life?

D·A·Y 5
SPIRITUAL REFRESHMENT

THINK ON THESE THINGS

Today is a day for spiritual refreshment. It's a day to slowly digest the Word of God. It's a day to praise and thank Him for His many blessings upon my life.

He who forms the mountains, creates the wind, and reveals his thoughts to man, he who turns dawn to darkness, and treads the high places of the earth – the LORD God Almighty is his name.

~ Amos 4:13

It's very easy to fall into step with the world's thinking and put on the world's attitudes about life. When our lives fail to embrace discipline and our desires become selfish, it's time to stop and reevaluate our lives.

For as he thinketh in his heart, so is he.

~ *Proverbs 23:7 KJV*

SPIRITUAL
REFRESHMENT

FAITH'S ACTION:
*It's time to stop and
reevaluate our lives.*
Take time out to
assess where you've
come from and
where you're going.
Are you still on
the road that will
lead you to God's
purposes, or have
you taken a detour
somewhere along
the way?

D·A·Y 6
COUNT YOUR BLESSINGS

THINK ON THESE THINGS

Only as we stop in meditation will our hearts be filled with praise for our friends, our past blessings, and our God. A thankful heart is one that has time to count blessings.

You will eat the fruit of your labor; blessings and prosperity will be yours.

~ Psalm 128:2

Relaxation and rest are necessary that we might feel, think, and act right.

*Blessed be the
Lord, who daily
loadeth us with
benefits, even
the God of
our salvation.*
~ *Psalm 68:19, KJV*

He makes me lie down in green pastures, he leads me beside quiet waters, he restores my soul. He guides me in paths of righteousness for his name's sake.

~ *Psalm 23:2-3*

FAITH'S ACTION:
Count your blessings, name them one by one, count your blessings, and it will surprise you what the Lord has done.

D·A·Y 7
HANDS OF LOVE

THINK ON THESE THINGS

The beauty of genuine concern is its willingness to become involved without being influenced by the price tag.

_____

_____

_____

_____

_____

_____

_____

_____

_____

_____

And God is able to make all grace abound to you, so that in all things at all times, having all that you need, you will abound in every good work.

~ 2 Corinthians 9:8

Love has hands to help others. It has feet to hasten to the poor and needy. It has eyes to see the hurts of the world. It has lips to encourage those in despair.

Love always protects, always trusts, always hopes, always perseveres. Love never fails (1 Cor. 13:7-8).

Jesus was concerned that people see the needs of humanity and respond with care.

Then he said to his disciples, "The harvest is plentiful but the workers are few. Ask the Lord of the harvest, therefore, to send out workers into his harvest field."
~ Matthew 9:37-38

FAITH'S ACTION:
If I'm to say to my world, "I couldn't care more," I must open my eyes and look for hurting people.

D·A·Y 8
UNCOMMON RESPONSES

THINK ON THESE THINGS

Only by taking time to reflect on yesterday and honestly evaluate its successes and failures can you learn and prepare for tomorrow.

I remember the days of long ago; I meditate on all your works and consider what your hands have done.

~ Psalm 143:5

Jesus' uncommon response to the everyday problems caused those around Him to ask, "What manner of man is this?"

Brokenheartedness? An opportunity to comfort. Disease? An opportunity to heal. Hatred? An opportunity to love. Sin? An opportunity to forgive.

His divine power has given us everything we need for life and godliness through our knowledge of him who called us by his own glory and goodness. Through these he has given us his very great and precious promises, so that through them you may participate in the divine nature and escape the corruption in the world caused by evil desires. For this very reason, make every effort to add to your faith goodness; and to goodness, knowledge; and to knowledge, self-control; and to self-control, perseverance; and to perseverance, godliness; and to godliness, brotherly kindness; and to brotherly kindness, love. For if you possess these qualities in increasing measure, they will keep you from being ineffective and unproductive in your knowledge of our Lord Jesus Christ.

~ 2 Peter 1:3-8

FAITH'S ACTION:
Father God, help me to become more like You, to see the problems around me today as opportunities to reach out in love to those who are in need. Amen.

D·A·Y 9
WORKERS IN GOD'S KINGDOM

THINK ON THESE THINGS

Unquestionably, God's Kingdom is being advanced by people of little talent doing little jobs for a big God.

Not that I have already obtained all this, or have already been made perfect, but I press on to take hold of that for which Christ Jesus took hold of me. Brothers, I do not consider myself yet to have taken hold of it. But one thing I do: Forgetting what is behind and straining toward what is ahead, I press on toward the goal to win the prize for which God has called me heavenward in Christ Jesus.

~ Philippians 3:12-14

No longer is it a question of, "How can I expand my potential?" but rather "How can I allow God's power to flow through me?"

_____

_____

_____

_____

_____

_____

_____

_____

_____

_____

_____

Your willingness to learn and adjust positively from mistakes and short-comings will largely determine how far you will travel the road to success.

For we are God's workmanship, created in Christ Jesus to do good works, which God prepared in advance for us to do.

~ Ephesians 2:10

FAITH'S ACTION:
How can I allow
God's power to flow
through me?

D·A·Y 10
OVERCOMING PROBLEMS

THINK ON THESE THINGS

Problems will begin to resolve more easily when exposed to the light of time. It's always best to give tough situations extra time for creative thinking and effective action.

Therefore do not worry about tomorrow, for tomorrow will worry about itself. Each day has enough trouble of its own.

~ Matthew 6:34

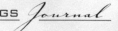
Part of the preparation for the battles of life is not only to acquire the right equipment to wear on the body but also to make proper preparations of the mind. "Hold still" before charging into the activities of life.

In addition to all this, take up the shield of faith, with which you can extinguish all the flaming arrows of the evil one. Take the helmet of salvation and the sword of the Spirit, which is the word of God. And pray in the Spirit on all occasions with all kinds of prayers and requests.
~ Ephesians 6:16-18

Our spiritual, physical, and emotional condition will greatly determine how we react to situations. The better we feel, the more capable we will be to evaluate difficult situations and make important decisions. When pressures are pressing, schedules are screaming, and the world is whirling, don't just do something – stand there!

Therefore put on the full armor of God, so that when the day of evil comes, you may be able to stand your ground, and after you have done everything, to stand. Stand firm then.

~ *Ephesians 6:13-14*

FAITH'S ACTION:
Every problem
becomes an
opportunity for
God to move.

S·E·C·T·I·O·N 2

POINTERS
ON POTENTIAL

In him we were also chosen, having been
predestined according to the plan of him who
works out everything in conformity with the purpose
of his will, in order that we, who were the first to
hope in Christ, might be for the praise of his glory.
Ephesians 1:11-12

D·A·Y 11
FULL POTENTIAL

THINK ON THESE THINGS

If you're a Christian then you must not be content until you develop to the fullest extent the potential God has given you.

For we are God's workmanship, created in Christ Jesus to do good works, which God prepared in advance for us to do.

~ _Ephesians 2:10_

Great people are ordinary people with an extraordinary amount of determination.

Christ in you, the hope of glory.

~ *Colossians 1:27*

FAITH'S ACTION:

Every person has hidden potential. No one has ever become all he or she can become. What undeveloped potential can you begin to develop today?

D·A·Y 12
BETTER THAN AVERAGE

THINK ON THESE THINGS

Every person needs that faith which will light any path, relieve any distress, bring joy out of sorrow, peace out of strife, and friendship out of enmity.

When you possess that faith, you'll be used of God to light the path of those who stumble, encourage the hearts of those who faint, relieve the load of those whose burdens are heavy; and plant a song in the hearts of those who are sad.

We continually remember before our God and Father your work produced by faith, your labor prompted by love, and your endurance inspired by hope in our Lord Jesus Christ.

~ 1 Thessalonians 1:3

You'll never be "just average" if you're a Christian, because you possess more determination, faith, and love than the average person.

And now these three remain: faith, hope and love. But the greatest of these is love.

~ *1 Corinthians 13:13*

FAITH'S ACTION:
How is your
faith visible in
your daily life?

D·A·Y 13
LOOK TO THE FUTURE

THINK ON THESE THINGS

Leaders in all areas of life have distinguishing characteristics.
One characteristic common to all is vision.

Where there is no vision, the people perish.

~ _Proverbs 29:18, KJV_

Leaders see life as it could be. They are always seeing a little farther, a little more, than those around them.

Many good people with a lot of potential are going nowhere because they have no dream.

And afterward, I will pour out my Spirit on all people. Your sons and daughters will prophesy, your old men will dream dreams, your young men will see visions.
~ Joel 2:28

A good dream is like cream – it will lift you to the top.

FAITH'S ACTION:
Successful people have a dream that becomes too exciting, too important to remain in the realm of fantasy. Their dream becomes a burning desire.

D·A·Y 14
NOTHING IS IMPOSSIBLE

THINK ON THESE THINGS

When people have the same spirit expressed by the apostle Paul – "I can do all things through him who gives me strength" (Phil. 4:13) – they're going to go over the top in all areas of life.

But thanks be to God, who always leads us in triumphal procession in Christ and through us spreads everywhere the fragrance of the knowledge of him.

~ 2 Corinthians 2:14

No matter what field of endeavor we're pursuing, those of us who throw our hearts into our work will know success.

Whatever you do, work at it with all your heart, as working for the Lord, not for men.

~ *Colossians 3:23*

FAITH'S ACTION:
Remember, success does not come from your efforts alone – but from drawing on the strength of the Lord. Pray that He will fill you with His strength to accomplish His plan for your life.

D·A·Y 15
REACHING NEW HEIGHTS

THINK ON THESE THINGS

Success takes growth and development. It's achieving one thing and using that as a stepping stone to rise higher up the mountain of accomplishment.

The Sovereign LORD is my strength; he makes my feet like the feet of a deer, he enables me to go on the heights.

~ *Habakkuk 3:19*

To keep changing is not an end in itself, but only through change can there be true growth. Every growing organism grows to maturity, levels off, and dies, unless there's new life, new blood, new activity, and new ideas.

Moment by
moment,
experiences
of growth and
adventure in
walking by faith
can be ours.

Then we will no longer be infants, tossed back and forth by the waves, and blown here and there by every wind of teaching and by the cunning and crafti- ness of men in their deceitful scheming. Instead, speaking the truth in love, we will in all things grow up into him who is the Head, that is, Christ.
~ Ephesians 4:14-15

FAITH'S ACTION:
What new life,
new blood, new
activity, and new
ideas are keeping
your life growing?

D·A·Y 16
OVERCOMING OBSTACLES

THINK ON THESE THINGS

A successful person is one who takes the cold water dumped on his or her plans, heats it with enthusiasm, and manufactures the steam that helps him or her push ahead.

Let us not become weary in doing good, for at the proper time we will reap a harvest if we do not give up.

~ Galatians 6:9

Many people see such a large problem in front of them that they're unable to comprehend the possibility of either overcoming or avoiding that particular obstacle. What big barriers frustrate you and cause you to believe that your goals are impossible and unreachable? What negative note causes discord in your dreams or causes them to go flat or turn sour?

"I have told you these things, so that in me you may have peace. In this world you will have trouble. But take heart! I have overcome the world."

~ John 16:33

FAITH'S ACTION:
Take the obstacles
that seem to be
blocking your path,
and see how they
can be turned into
stepping stones.

Remember: ability is 95% "stickability."

D·A·Y 17
DARE TO DREAM

THINK ON THESE THINGS

Today you may not be what you want to be, or dream of becoming, but the one key to achieving your dream is determining not to quit.

The LORD will fulfill his purpose for me; your love, O LORD, endures forever – do not abandon the works of your hands.

~ *Psalm 138:8*

To rise above the common plane of living you need a little more determination than the average person.

Success is achieved and maintained by those who keep trying.

He who began a good work in you will carry it on to completion until the day of Christ Jesus.

~ *Philippians 1:6*

Until a person has tried hard enough and long enough to get his "second wind," he'll never know how much he can accomplish.

We have come to share in Christ if we hold firmly till the end the confidence we had at first.

~ *Hebrews 3:14*

FAITH'S ACTION:
A dream plus
determination leads
to success.

D·A·Y 18
THE LORD LIFTS YOU UP

THINK ON THESE THINGS

We sometimes become careless and get in a hurry. Many times this happens just before we meet our goal. It looks as though we've been successful. The obstacles have been overcome. The sweet smell of victory permeates the air. But then ...

Sometimes inexperience causes us to fall. Sometimes lack of preparation is the problem. Maybe the problem is overconfidence.

The LORD upholds all those who fall and lifts up all who are bowed down.

~ *Psalm 145:14*

If we become involved with life and become players instead of spectators, the obstacles of life will sometimes trip us.

The difference between success and failure is how we react after the fall. Remember: the failure is *not* in the fall. The failure is in allowing the fall to keep us down and to control our lives.

But you are a shield around me, O LORD; *you bestow glory on me and lift up my head.*
~ Psalm 3:3

For though a righteous man falls seven times, he rises again, but the wicked are brought down by calamity.

~ *Proverbs 24:16*

D·A·Y 18

THE LORD
LIFTS YOU UP

FAITH'S ACTION:
The failure is not in the fall. Many times, things that look like apparent failures help to give new perspective on old problems. Use them to redefine your goals and realign your potential.

D·A·Y 19
FLY LIKE AN EAGLE

THINK ON THESE THINGS

What a thrill to know that there's a power from God that will help us attain spiritual heights as the eagle attains physical heights.

Do you not know? Have you not heard? The LORD is the everlasting God, the Creator of the ends of the earth. He will not grow tired or weary, and his understanding no one can fathom. He gives strength to the weary and increases the power of the weak. Even youths grow tired and weary, and young men stumble and fall; but those who hope in the LORD will renew their strength. They will soar on wings like eagles; they will run and not grow weary, they will walk and not be faint.

~ Isaiah 40:28-31

Like the eagles we can choose to keep our eyes on the heights. Slowly, steadily, with determination, we can pass the "sparrow's nest."

_____

_____

_____

_____

_____

_____

_____

_____

God has designed
and empowered
us to be like the
eagle. Each day it's
possible to reach
another unknown
height.

A feeling of
exhilaration surges
through you when
you know you've
done everything
possible to fulfill
the potential God
has given you.

*Everyone born of God overcomes the world. This is the victory that has overcome
the world, even our faith.*

~ 1 John 5:4

FAITH'S ACTION:
Keep your eyes on
the heights and you
will soar to new
heights.

D·A·Y 20
THE POWER OF POTENTIAL

THINK ON THESE THINGS

You and your talents are not an accident. You are special in God's eyes. You have distinct gifts and talents. You have shoes to fill that no one else can wear.

Trust in the LORD with all your heart and lean not on your own understanding; in all your ways acknowledge him, and he will make your paths straight.

~ _Proverbs 3:5-6_

Inside you is enormous potential just waiting to be developed and put to use. Since God created you for a purpose, it's only with God that you can become what He intends.

"For I know the plans I have for you," declares the LORD, *"plans to prosper you and not to harm you, plans to give you hope and a future."*

~ *Jeremiah 29:11*

God's gift to you
is your potential.
What you do
with it is your gift
to God. He is
concerned not only
about what you are
but about what you
can become.

*In the same way, let your light shine before men, that they may see your good deeds
and praise your Father in heaven.*

~ Matthew 5:16

FAITH'S ACTION:
How can your
potential be used
for the greater glory
of the Kingdom of
God?

S·E·C·T·I·O·N 3

SUCCESS

Blessed is the man who does not walk in the counsel of the wicked or stand in the way of sinners or sit in the seat of mockers. But his delight is in the law of the LORD, and on his law he meditates day and night. He is like a tree planted by streams of water, which yields its fruit in season and whose leaf does not wither. Whatever he does prospers.

Psalm 1:1-3

D·A·Y 21
MEETING NEEDS

THINK ON THESE THINGS

Success is choosing to enter the arena of action, determined to give yourself to the cause that will better humanity and last for eternity.

Use the things of the world, as if not engrossed in them. For this world in its present form is passing away.

~ *1 Corinthians 7:31*

The Good Samaritan vividly illustrates the difference between a winner and a loser. He not only saw the need, but endeavored to meet it.

We're not successful until we know what's right and then do it.

But a Samaritan, as
he traveled, came
where the man was;
and when he saw
him, he took pity on
him. He went to him
and bandaged his
wounds, pouring on
oil and wine. Then
he put the man on
his own donkey, took
him to an inn and
took care of him.
~ Luke 10:33-34

The way to the top is not "stepping on others" but "stooping to help others."

_____

_____

_____

_____

_____

FAITH'S ACTION:
How do you define
success in your life?

_____

_____

_____

_____

_____

_____

_____

_____

D·A·Y 22
REACHING GOALS

THINK ON THESE THINGS

Success is having a plan and following it.

And the LORD answered me, and said, Write the vision, and make it plain upon tables, that he may run that readeth it. For the vision is yet for an appointed time, but at the end it shall speak, and not lie: though it tarry, wait for it; because it will surely come, it will not tarry.

~ _Habakkuk 2:2-3_ KJV

It's easy to see what an individual is pursuing in his or her goals for life. The way the person undertakes his or her affairs is largely determined by the way the person sees his or her goals.

> God has
> created you
> for a purpose.

Therefore I do not run like a man running aimlessly; I do not fight like a man beating the air.

~ *1 Corinthians 9:26*

FAITH'S ACTION:
Are you excited
as you pursue the
goals that you and
God have set?

D·A·Y 23
INVEST YOUR TALENTS

THINK ON THESE THINGS

The more I have studied the parable of the talents and observed those people who have lived lives of giving to others, the more I have come to the conclusion that it's impossible to lose what you share with others.

The man who had received the five talents went at once and put his money to work and gained five more. So also, the one with the two talents gained two more.

~ Matthew 25:16-17

Success is
developing a talent
and sharing it,
not merely having
talents.

Those who share
and invest their
talents, regardless
of the number,
increase and
develop them.

Freely you have received, freely give.

~ *Matthew 10:8*

FAITH'S ACTION:
In what ways can
your talents be used
for God's glory?

D·A·Y 24
THE FRUIT OF SUCCESS

THINK ON THESE THINGS

No amount of genius, talent, finesse, or "right connections" will ever bring the fruit of success without a real commitment. Commitment is the motivator that keeps a person moving toward his or her goal. Commitment gets you started while others stand, and keeps you going while others quit.

He who works his land will have abundant food, but he who chases fantasies lacks judgment.

~ Proverbs 12:11

Every great commitment has a price tag. The greater the job, the higher the price. That price tag is known as commitment. The level of your determination to accomplish your work is measured by what it takes to make you quit.

All hard work brings a profit, but mere talk leads only to poverty.

~ *Proverbs 14:23*

Always give yourselves fully to the work of the Lord, because you know that your labor in the Lord is not in vain.

~ 1 Corinthians 15:58

FAITH'S ACTION:
Make a commitment to commit yourself to achieving your goals.

D·A·Y 25
THE PERFECT WILL OF GOD

THINK ON THESE THINGS

The only security for the believer is not found in avoiding battles, temptations, and problems, but in *being found in the perfect will of God.*

The children of Israel would have been more secure fighting giants in Canaan than wandering in the wilderness.

"My food," said Jesus, "is to do the will of him who sent me and to finish his work."
~ *John 4:34*

D·A·Y 25

THE PERFECT
WILL OF GOD

The importance of making proper decisions in life is illustrated in the lives of the children of Israel at Kadesh-barnea. As they came to the point that called for a decision, they began to waver. They looked at God in the light of their circumstances instead of the possibilities. They were more influenced by the size of men than the size of God.

*Then Caleb
silenced the people
before Moses and
said, "We should
go up and take
possession of the
land, for we can
certainly do it."*
~ Numbers 13:30

FAITH'S ACTION:
Bring any decisions
that you need to
make before God
in prayer, and trust
Him.

D·A·Y 26
PLAN WELL

THINK ON THESE THINGS

The plans established for any endeavor will greatly determine the end result. Remember – nothing will ever be accomplished if you wait for everyone's approval or for the plan to be perfect. No plan eliminates all problems. Excellent planning will remove some obstacles, but not all of them.

Commit your way to the LORD; trust in him and he will do this: He will make your righteousness shine like the dawn, the justice of your cause like the noonday sun.
~ Psalm 37:5-6

Well-defined
goals very
quickly expose
activities that
are hindering
progress
toward certain
objectives.

Many are the plans in a man's heart, but it is the LORD's purpose that prevails.
~ *Proverbs 19:21*

FAITH'S ACTION:
Plan ahead.

D·A·Y 27
CONFIDENCE AND STRENGTH

THINK ON THESE THINGS

Nothing builds confidence like pointing to yesterday's victories. Nothing gives strength like knowing that what was done yesterday can be accomplished again today.

Blessed are all who fear the LORD, who walk in his ways. You will eat the fruit of your labor; blessings and prosperity will be yours.

~ Psalm 128:1-2

Change affects emotions, and logic seldom wins in the arena of emotionalism. The barrier of ignorance must be crossed. The walls of insecurity must be climbed. The ceilings of the unimaginative must be lifted.

New challenges will arise. New questions will be asked. New solutions must be sought.

> "Forget the former
> things; do not dwell
> on the past. See, I am
> doing a new thing!
> Now it springs up; do
> you not perceive it?"
> ~ Isaiah 43:18-19

**CONFIDENCE
AND STRENGTH**

FAITH'S ACTION:
Check daily to make
sure you're still
on target. If not,
make the needed
adjustments, and
continue on toward
success.

D·A·Y 28
A VISION OF VICTORY

THINK ON THESE THINGS

A victory begins with a vision. A vision of winning – a vision of going over the top. The people who constantly rise to the top are those who possess a vision *before* the prize is won. They see the triumph before anyone else. The winner is the one who can work harder for longer periods of time *without quitting.*

_____

_____

_____

_____

_____

_____

_____

But one thing I do: Forgetting what is behind and straining toward what is ahead, I press on toward the goal to win the prize for which God has called me heavenward in Christ Jesus.

~ Philippians 3:13-14

The thrill of victory comes only when a stated objective has been reached. No target, no thrill!

"His master replied, 'Well done, good and faithful servant! You have been faithful with a few things; I will put you in charge of many things. Come and share your master's happiness!'"

~ Matthew 25:21

FAITH'S ACTION:

*Delight yourself
in the Lord and
he will give
you the desires of
your heart.*
~ Psalm 37:4

D·A·Y 29
SEIZE THE DAY

THINK ON THESE THINGS

Only *you* have the power to determine the sacrifice, energy, and time that *you* will supply to become a winner.

_____

_____

_____

_____

_____

_____

_____

_____

_____

How long will you lie there, you sluggard? When will you get up from your sleep? A little sleep, a little slumber, a little folding of the hands to rest – and poverty will come on you like a bandit and scarcity like an armed man.

~ Proverbs 6:9-11

One thing worse
than not having
life options open
to you is having
open opportunities
and not taking
advantage of them.
You're the only
person who can
determine to seize
the opportunities
of the moment.

*Be very careful,
then, how you live –
not as unwise but
as wise, making the
most of every
opportunity, because
the days are evil.*
~ Ephesians 5:15-16

FAITH'S ACTION:
Carpe Diem – How
will you make
the most of your
opportunities today?

D·A·Y 30
A BEND IN THE ROAD

THINK ON THESE THINGS

You may need some type of a roadblock to be placed in front of your progress so that your physical, emotional, or spiritual well-being can become properly balanced for the road you're to travel.

The steps of a good man are ordered by the LORD: and he delighteth in his way.
~ *Psalm 37:23, KJV*

Some of your greatest moments can be times when you're forced out of a rut because of a turn of events.

But if we hope for what we do not yet have, we wait for it patiently.

~ *Romans 8:25*

Disappointments
are only delays.
What cannot be
enjoyed today will
possibly be yours
tomorrow.

So do not throw away your confidence; it will be richly rewarded. You need to persevere so that when you have done the will of God, you will receive what he has promised.

~ *Hebrews 10:35-36*

FAITH'S ACTION:
Valuable lessons
freely flow our
way when our
plans are denied
or postponed.

S·E·C·T·I·O·N 4

LOOK OUT FOR
YOUR LOOKOUT

Since, then, you have been raised with Christ,
set your hearts on things above, where Christ is
seated at the right hand of God. Set your minds
on things above, not on earthly things.
Colossians 3:1-2

D·A·Y 31
THE CONTENTED PERSON

THINK ON THESE THINGS

The contented person has surrendered to a purpose that demands his or her best; the discontented person has selfishly hoarded much, and grasping for more, will not rest.

One man gives freely, yet gains even more; another withholds unduly, but comes to poverty.

~ _Proverbs 11:24_

The contented person has placed his or her values on things that will forever last; the discontented person has placed his or her values on things that will soon be past.

The contented person counts his or her blessings and names them one by one; the discontented person counts others' blessings and thinks he or she has no fun.

*From the fullness of
his grace we have all
received one blessing
after another.*
~ John 1:16

FAITH'S ACTION:
God has created
you to fulfill a
special purpose
that no one else
can.

D·A·Y 32
SUCCESS IN CHRIST

THINK ON THESE THINGS

Paul knew the secret of success was not self-confidence but *Christ*-confidence. His achievements could only come through Christ, and he succeeded because in every problem he remembered this truth.

So do not fear, for I am with you; do not be dismayed, for I am your God. I will strengthen you and help you; I will uphold you with my righteous right hand.

~ Isaiah 41:10

Sooner or later a person, if he or she is wise, discovers that life is a mixture of good and bad days, victory and defeat, give and take.

But now, this is what the LORD says – he who created you, O Jacob, he who formed you, O Israel: "Fear not, for I have redeemed you; I have summoned you by name; you are mine. When you pass through the waters, I will be with you; and when you pass through the rivers, they will not sweep over you. When you walk through the fire, you will not be burned; the flames will not set you ablaze."

~ Isaiah 43:1-2

FAITH'S ACTION:

If any of you lack wisdom, he should ask God, who gives generously to all without finding fault, and it will be given to him.
~ James 1:5

D·A·Y 33
REACHING OUT

THINK ON THESE THINGS

When we begin to forget ourselves by reaching out to others, a spirit of usefulness and encouragement invades our lives.

And let us consider how we may spur one another on toward love and good deeds. Let us not give up meeting together, as some are in the habit of doing, but let us encourage one another – and all the more as you see the Day approaching.

~ Hebrews 10:24-25

There is no more effective way of overcoming discouragement than by sharing something good with someone.

> *And God is able to make all grace abound to you, so that in all things at all times, having all that you need, you will abound in every good work.*
> ~ 2 Corinthians 9:8

FAITH'S ACTION:
Right now, decide right where you live that you're going to be an encourager, an uplifter, and a helper.

D·A·Y 34
STEPPING STONES

THINK ON THESE THINGS

Hope is holding on when things around you begin to slip away. Hope is praying expectantly when there seemingly are no answers. The only difference between those who threw in the towel and quit and those who used their energy to rebuild and kept going is found in the word "hope."

May the God of hope fill you with all joy and peace as you trust in him, so that you may overflow with hope by the power of the Holy Spirit.

~ Romans 15:13

Disappointments are stepping stones. Victorious is that person who knows how to make stepping stones out of stumbling stones. As each stone is placed on our pathway to the top, it will either become a help or a hindrance, depending on how we handle each situation. Climb on top of each stone and go toward a higher victory.

Therefore, I urge you, brothers, in view of God's mercy, to offer your bodies as living sacrifices, holy and pleasing to God – this is your spiritual act of worship. Do not conform any longer to the pattern of this world, but be transformed by the renewing of your mind. Then you will be able to test and approve what God's will is – his good, pleasing and perfect will.

~ Romans 12:1-2

FAITH'S ACTION:
How can your
stumbling stones
be turned into
stepping stones?

D·A·Y 35
LIFE'S GREATEST VIRTUES

THINK ON THESE THINGS

How you act toward life shows what type of person you want to be. How you react toward life shows what type of person you are right now. Successful people realize that the door to the room of success swings on the hinges of setbacks and opposition.

Consider it pure joy, my brothers, whenever you face trials of many kinds, because you know that the testing of your faith develops perseverance. Perseverance must finish its work so that you may be mature and complete, not lacking anything. If any of you lacks wisdom, he should ask God, who gives generously to all without finding fault, and it will be given to him.

~ James 1:2-5

There's no possible way that the fruit of maturity can be in evidence in your life without your experiencing disappointments. Some of life's greatest virtues – such as faith, patience, perseverance, and hope – come by way of disappointments.

Not only so, but we also rejoice in our sufferings, because we know that suffering produces perseverance; perseverance, character; and character, hope.

~ *Romans 5:3-4*

FAITH'S ACTION:
What type of person are you? What type of person do you want to be?

D·A·Y 36
THIS NEW DAY

THINK ON THESE THINGS

Monday is the beginning of a new venture – it's the start of another journey. Monday gives me an opportunity to dream new dreams and set new goals. Monday is the day I enter into the arena of action. It's time to see if my game plan will really work.

The path of the righteous is like the first gleam of dawn, shining ever brighter till the full light of day.

~ Proverbs 4:18

Monday morning is the only time I can stand up and say, "So far this week I haven't made a mistake."

*Because of the LORD's
great love we are not
consumed, for his
compassions never fail.
They are new every
morning; great
is your faithfulness.*
~ Lamentations 3:22-23

FAITH'S ACTION:

*This is the day the
LORD has made;
let us rejoice and
be glad in it.
~ Psalm 118:24*

D·A·Y 37
OPPORTUNITY KNOCKS

THINK ON THESE THINGS

Opportunities for success in this world are as great as we have the imagination to dream them, but we can't see them when we're down on ourselves and the world. Don't feel sorry for yourself if you're limited in your abilities and talents. The world is full of opportunities behind closed doors so start knocking.

"Ask and it will be given to you; seek and you will find; knock and the door will be opened to you. For everyone who asks receives; he who seeks finds; and to him who knocks, the door will be opened."

~ *Matthew 7:7-8*

I am not totally convinced that all is lost if we allow an opportunity to pass us by without seizing it. Opportunities will come again to give us a second chance to achieve our goal.

Opportunities come more than once if we're willing to try other avenues to reach our goal.

Whether you turn to the right or to the left, your ears will hear a voice behind you, saying, "This is the way; walk in it."

~ Isaiah 30:21

FAITH'S ACTION:
Keep your
eyes open for
opportunities
behind closed
doors.

D·A·Y 38
PERSISTENT VICTORY

THINK ON THESE THINGS

Victory does not usually go to the most skilled. Victory is usually won by those who are the most persistent.

_____

_____

_____

_____

_____

_____

_____

_____

_____

_____

_____

And we know that in all things God works for the good of those who love him, who have been called according to his purpose.

~ Romans 8:28

It almost seems that great success is won only by people who overcome incredible obstacles and great discouragement. Success is achieved and maintained by those who keep trying.

Regardless of the goal, a persistent effort is one of the most important ingredients for personal success.

And we pray this in order that you may live a life worthy of the Lord and may please him in every way: bearing fruit in every good work, growing in the knowledge of God, being strengthened with all power according to his glorious might so that you may have great endurance and patience.

~ Colossians 1:10-11

FAITH'S ACTION:
Your expectations must not be based on what you are today, but on what you hope to become someday.

D·A·Y 39
AFTER DARK, THE DAWN

THINK ON THESE THINGS

The true test of persistence comes when the night is the darkest. Only when the answers fade away, leaving only problems, and when the moral support of others disappears and loneliness becomes our partner can the strength of our persistence be determined.

For God did not give us a spirit of timidity, but a spirit of power, of love and of self-discipline.

~ 2 Timothy 1:7

Sometimes, prospects may seem dimmest just when they're on the turn. A little more persistence, a little more effort, and what seemed a hopeless failure may turn into a glorious success.

*Even in darkness
light dawns for
the upright, for
the gracious
and compassionate
and righteous man.
~ Psalm 112:4*

FAITH'S ACTION:
The better we
understand the
problems, the
greater our chance
of victory.

D·A·Y 40
STRENGTH FOR TOMORROW

THINK ON THESE THINGS

Only by taking time to reflect on yesterday and honestly evaluate its successes and failures can you learn and prepare for tomorrow.

Let us hold unswervingly to the hope we profess, for he who promised is faithful.
~ Hebrews 10:23

Opportunities for success in this world are as great as we have the imagination to dream them.

Finally, be strong in the Lord and in his mighty power.

~ Ephesians 6:10

What a difference
it makes to
realize that to be
connected to God
means His power is
our power!

Now to him who is able to do immeasurably more than all we ask or imagine, according to his power that is at work within us, to him be glory in the church and in Christ Jesus throughout all generations, for ever and ever! Amen.

~ Ephesians 3:20-21

STRENGTH FOR
TOMORROW

FAITH'S ACTION:
Forget your past
failures and begin
to enlarge your
expectations for
tomorrow.